SEASONED
with
SALT

Other Books by David Roper
  A Burden Shared
  Elijah: A Man Like Us
  Growing Slowly Wise
  In Quietness and Confidence
  Jacob: The Fools God Chooses
  A Man to Match the Mountain
  Out of the Ordinary
  Psalm 23: The Song of a Passionate Heart
  The Strength of a Man

SEASONED
with
SALT

DAVID ROPER

Discovery House Publishers

Books, music, and videos that feed the soul with the Word of God

Box 3566 Grand Rapids, MI 49501

Discovery House Publishers is affiliated with RBC Ministries, Grand Rapids, Michigan 49512.

Discovery House books are distributed to the trade exclusively by Barbour Publishing, Inc., Uhrichsville, Ohio 44683.

Book design and composition by Lakeside Design Plus.

Requests for permission to quote from this book should be directed to: Permissions Department, Discovery House Publishers, P.O. Box 3566, Grand Rapids, MI 49501.

"When at length" by Ruth Bell Graham from *Sitting by My Laughing Fire* is used by permission of Ruth Bell Graham.

In retelling the portion of Elisha's story found in a particular chapter's warm-up reading, biblical conversations and quotes, though not cited by verse number, are direct quotes from *The New International Version,* unless indicated otherwise. The New International Version (NIV), © 1973, 1978, 1984 by the International Bible Society, is used by permission of Zondervan Bible Publishers.

Library of Congress Cataloging-in-Publication
  Roper, David, 1933-
    Seasoned with salt : lessons from Elisha / by David Roper
        p. cm.
      ISBN 1-57293-129-9
        1. Elisha (Biblical prophet)—Meditations. 2. Christian life.
    3. Meditations. I. Title.

  BS580.E5R67 2004
  222'.54092—dc22

                                                          2004010675

  Printed in United States of America
  04 05 06 07 08 09 / / 10 9 8 7 6 5 4 3 2 1

contents

INTRODUCTION: THIN PLACES

And a great hand reached out of the dark, and grasped mine for a moment, mightily and tenderly. I said to myself, "The veil between, though very dark, is very thin."

—GEORGE MACDONALD, *PHANTASTES*

I t's tempting to summarize Elisha's ministry as "The Miraculous Works of Elisha," for more miracles are attributed to him than almost any other person in the Bible. Our Lord Jesus is the sole exception.

You can look at Elisha's miracles in several ways. Some would say they were mere manifestations of authority and power. The argument goes something like this: God wanted to show us what a great man Elisha was and so permitted him to do things that no other human being could do.

That may be true in part, but it's not the whole.

Others see Elisha's miracles as a part of a "Baal polemic," Elisha's effort to establish that Yahweh, Israel's God, is greater than the gods and goddesses of Canaan. There's truth in that assessment as well.

A third way to look at Elisha's miracles is to see each one as a "breakthrough," a moment in time when God reaches out of the unseen realm of eternity and into time. They are the "thin places" in the universe, as Celtic Christians used to say, where for a moment we catch a glimpse of God, revealing, in each case, something of His power, His compassion, His passion to reach out and touch us with His love. We see Him caring, cherishing, nourishing, nurturing, encouraging. "The lesson of them," George MacDonald said, "is that help is always within God's reach when His children want it."

It's hard, if not impossible, to love raw power. We can only fear it, as Dorothy and her friends feared the Great Oz. But when we see

9

that Love is behind all the power in the universe, when we see God using His power for our contentment, our joy, our peace of mind, we are awed and our hearts are filled with affection for Him.

I like to put it this way: Miracles are *vignettes*—little pictures of God. They correct our distortions and undo our misconceptions, because we see God as He *really* is.

I read a story once about a little boy who was busy drawing a picture of God. "But," his mother gently chided, "no one has seen God. We don't know what He looks like."

"We will when I get through," the boy replied.

This, I pray, will be the fruit of these chapters.[1]

DAVID ROPER

BOISE, IDAHO

---

1. I'm reluctant to try to explain each miracle-parable, for each must stand on its own. To explain them is to explain them away, like explaining a joke to someone who doesn't get it. We "murder to dissect," Wordsworth said. In "The Fantastic Imagination," George MacDonald wrote, "I say again, if I cannot draw a horse, I will not write THIS IS A HORSE under what I foolishly meant for one. Any key to a work of imagination would be nearly, if not quite, as absurd. The tale is there, not to hide, but to show: if it shows nothing at your window, do not open your door to it; leave it out in the cold. To ask me to explain, is to say, 'Roses! Boil them, or we won't have them!' My tales may not be roses but I will not boil them." MacDonald notwithstanding, I will wander into explanation and "boil" these miracle-parables from time to time to give you some idea of what I have seen. The rest I leave to you, to invite into your heart or to leave "out in the cold."

THE CALL

The mantle fell to the young prophet's part,
With double portion of his father's art.

—JOHN DRYDEN

2 Kings 2:1–12

The best stories begin with God: "The LORD said to him [Elijah], 'Go back the way you came, and go to the Desert of Damascus. When you get there, anoint Hazael king over Aram. Also, anoint Jehu son of Nimshi king over Israel, and anoint Elisha son of Shaphat from Abel Meholah to succeed you as prophet' " (1 Kings 19:15–16).

And so, aware that his work on earth was almost finished, the old prophet Elijah turned again toward the land of Israel, to the village of Abel Meholah.[1] The rest of 1 Kings 19 tells the story. There Elijah found Elisha, Shaphat's son, dutifully working the ground, "driving the twelfth" of twelve pairs of oxen, eating the dust of eleven plows that were turning the soil in front of him.

The old prophet slipped up behind the young man and cast his rough, camel-hair mantle over his shoulders and moved on. Not a word was spoken, but Elisha understood. "When a great teacher died," Sir John Malcolm wrote in his *History of Persia,* "he bequeathed his patched mantle to the disciple he most esteemed. . . . His mantle was his all and its transfer marked out his heir." The mantle was a symbol of Elisha's call to the prophetic office.

Elisha's response was immediate: He left his oxen and "set out to follow Elijah." Thus his work began.

---

1. I develop this account in more detail in my book *Elijah, a Man Like Us: How an Ordinary Person Can Make an Extraordinary Difference* (Discovery House Publishers).

For a time Elisha did little more than minister to the physical needs of the old prophet, "pour[ing] water on his hands," as the idiom puts it (2 Kings 3:11). It was a time of humble, obscure service. But he learned at the feet of his master. He listened well, determined to let none of Elijah's words fall to the ground.

In turn, Elijah ministered to Elisha, strengthening the young man's grip on God. The old man knew there was no better way to spend his last days.

But earthly things must come to an end, and God informed Elijah that He was calling him home. Elijah, knowing that his departure was imminent and determined to leave a lasting legacy, asked his disciple, "What can I do for you before I am taken from you?" It was a door flung wide open, a chancy *carte blanche*, yet Elijah knew that Elisha would not ask for anything that God would not bestow.

Elijah's confidence was well placed. Elisha's reply showed the stuff of which he was made. He sought neither prestige nor power but a "double portion" of Elijah's spirit.

What did Elisha want? To be considered Elijah's eldest son, heir to his influence and successor to his work, for the "double portion" was the inheritance of the firstborn son (Deuteronomy 21:17).

Elisha knew he would succeed Elijah in his work, but he knew he could not take on its responsibilities and face its perils without adequate resources. He was eager to seek the Spirit that had endowed the older prophet with power from on high, for Elisha knew that he was a mere man—weak and feckless apart from God. If he was to do the work God had called him to do, he must have all of God to do it.

Elijah replied, "If you see me when I am taken from you, it [the double portion] will be yours—otherwise not." There was nothing arbitrary in this test. It was utterly suitable, for God's work requires the ability to "see."

And so, "As they were walking along and talking together, suddenly a chariot of fire and horses of fire appeared and separated the two of them, and Elijah went up to heaven in a whirlwind. Elisha saw this and cried out, 'My father! My father! The chariots and horsemen of Israel!' And Elisha saw him no more."

Elijah's requirement that Elisha see his departure had to do with one's ability to see what cannot be seen. "Elijah was a man like us," James 5:17 says. His power came not from latent or inherent human ability, but because his eyes were fixed "on what is unseen" (2 Corinthians 4:18). That was the secret of his influence. The issue in Elijah's "test" was whether Elisha had learned that secret.

An ordinary man or woman standing in that place would have seen nothing but the sudden disappearance of the prophet. As F. B. Meyer noted in his book, *Elijah and the Secret of His Power,* "To senses dulled by passion or blinded by materialism, the space occupied by the flaming seraphim would have seemed devoid of any special interest and bare as the rest of the surrounding scenery." But Elisha, an extraordinary man, saw the invisible hosts of God. He had learned from Elijah to fix his eyes "on what is unseen." This was the secret of his enduring influence.

And so it is with us. There is a world that "lies around us like a cloud; a world we do not see," noted Harriet Beecher Stowe, another realm of reality, more actual, more substantial than anything we can see, hear, touch, taste, smell in this world. Faith is the means by which we gain access to this invisible world. It is to the spiritual realm what the five senses are to the natural; it is the means by which we grasp spiritual reality and bring it into the realm of our experience. Our goal, then, is to "grow eyes," to borrow a phrase from George MacDonald.

And how do we grow eyes?

Simply put, "seeing" is believing. Seeing is *faith,* pure and simple. "Faith is being . . . certain of what we do not see" (Hebrews 11:1). "By faith, [Moses] left Egypt, not fearing the king's anger; he persevered because he *saw him who is invisible*" (Hebrews 11:27, italics mine). Faith is the indispensable element in all our work for God. Without it we can do nothing.

Faith cannot be generated. It is a gift of God given in answer to prayer. Do you want to "see" God in all His glory? Pray that the eyes of your hearts may be enlightened that you may see . . . (Ephesians 1:18).

Faith grows as we feed on God's Word: "Faith comes from hearing the message, and the message is heard through the word of Christ" (Romans 10:17). Spiritual awareness is seeing everything through God's eyes, hearing with His ears. The test of our time in the Word of God is this: Has it enabled us to see?

Faith is the product of obedience. Our sense of God's presence is conditioned by the purity of our hearts. "What you see," C. S. Lewis wrote, "depends a good deal on . . . what sort of person you are." It is the pure in heart who "see God" (Matthew 5:8).

What's needed is an undivided and uncompromising devotion to Christ, singleness and simplicity of purpose to love Him and follow Him. "Purity of heart is to will one thing," Kierkegaard said, and that one thing is God's will. Uncontaminated devotion to Christ is the source of insight into the unseen world. It enables perceptions that others cannot achieve. Such men and women glimpse the workings of God where others detect *nothing*.

Lord, open our eyes that we may *see* . . . (see Psalm 119:18).

THE OLD PROPHET

It is not wrong to depend upon Elijah as long as God gives him to you, but remember the time will come when he will have to go; when he stands no more to you as your guide and leader, because God does not intend he should. You say— "I cannot go on without Elijah." God says you must.

—OSWALD CHAMBERS, *MY UTMOST FOR HIS HIGHEST*

2 Kings 2:13–18

Elisha "picked up the cloak [mantle] that had fallen from Elijah and went back and stood on the bank of the Jordan." Then he took the old ragged, moth-eaten cloak, the symbol of Elijah's prophetic office to which he succeeded, raised it overhead in imitation of Elijah's act and brought it down on the waters . . . and nothing happened!

It's not clear from most translations of the Bible, but the Hebrew text has two "smitings," one before and one after Elisha's question in verse 14. And the Hebrew suggests that the waters did not part as expected the first time. The Septuagint, an early Greek version of the Old Testament, translates and clarifies the text: "He took the cloak that had fallen from him and struck the water with it, and it was not divided." Elijah's mantle had failed.

"Where now is the LORD, the God of Elijah?" Elisha cried out in desperation. Good question!

How often have we raised that question when we've been deprived of a highly regarded, longstanding leader, and we stand face to face with some obstacle? (Often there's more despair than query in the question.) How can we go on, we ask, when our pastor, our teacher, our father is no longer here?

Although old prophets come and go, God remains. He takes His weary workers home, but He calls others to take their place, and He

19

fills and floods *them* with His power. If you ask where He is, He answers: "Once more I am with you—in *this* one."

Godly leaders go, but God stays and reminds us that He is at hand to do for us what He has done for others in the past and to do so in unique and wonderfully creative ways.

Elisha's power did not lie in imitation of his mentor. There was nothing in Elijah and peculiar to him that qualified him for the task that God had given him to do. There was no power in his mantle, his manner, or his methods. The prophet's power was the power of the living God.

And so Elisha, with faith and confidence restored (and it must be restored again and again), struck the water and "it divided to the right and to the left, and he crossed over."

A company of young prophets from Jericho saw the Jordan part and rightly concluded, "The spirit of Elijah is resting on Elisha." They went to meet him and bowed down before him. The sign was evidence that Elisha came in the spirit and power of Elijah.

But the young prophets had not yet learned their lesson. Let's "go and look for your master," they pled. "Perhaps the Spirit of the Lord has picked him up and set him down on some mountain or in some valley."

"No," Elisha replied. "Don't go." But they persisted until they wore him down. Whereupon they "sent fifty men, who searched for three days but did not find him." When they returned to Elisha, in Jericho, he responded, "Didn't I tell you not to go?"

The eye untrained by faith looks for something more tangible than the unseen God. It yearns for the physical presence of an older prophet, a former pastor or leader, some leftover from another age. But to do so is to put our confidence in the flesh. We should never think of others or ourselves as indispensable. No one is essential but God.

So often God raises up an individual to do a unique work in a special way and empowers her or him by His Spirit to do the work. Then that person writes a book, we read it, and copy its methods, believing that wisdom and power lie in that worker's manner and modus operandi. But that's humanism, for it makes a mere human being the measure of all things.

It's right to give honor to those who have gone before us and to learn from their words and deeds. The author of Hebrews reminds us to remember our leaders, especially those "who spoke the word of God" to us, and to "consider the outcome of their way of life," that is, the influence they had on others and on us. But we must not imitate their ways and means. There's no power in any of them. We must, rather, as the epistle instructs us, "imitate their *faith*" (Hebrews 13:7, italics mine).

"Where is the God of Elijah?" we ask. He is with us in the form of the new prophet and leader. "There are varieties of activities," says Paul—many ways to do ministry—"but it is . . . *God* who activates all of them in everyone" (1 Corinthians 12:6 NRSV, italics mine).

SEASONED WITH SALT

We need loving communication, we need the presence of the Spirit. That is why I do not believe in theologians who do not pray, who are not in humble communication of love with God. Neither do I believe in the existence of any human power to pass on authentic knowledge of God. Only God can speak about himself, and only the Holy Spirit, who is love, can communicate this knowledge to us.

—CARLO CARRETTO, *THE GOD WHO COMES*

2 Kings 2:19–22

✦

Iericho was an oasis of rich soil, palms, pomegranates, and fig trees in the midst of a vast desert. As the men of the city said, the city was "well situated." The source of Jericho's fertility was an enormous spring from which the citizens irrigated their fields. But, as they complained to Elisha, the water of the spring had become toxic, and their fields had become "sterile," to use their exact word.

The choice of the word *sterile* is intentional, a clue to the significance of this event, for the account is part of the aggressive attack against Baal that governed the prophet's actions throughout his ministry.

Baal worship was now the state religion of Israel, made so by its former queen Jezebel, an ardent missionary of the cult. She had established a Baal site at Jezreel, Israel's summer capital—supporting its 450 priests out of her own funds—and induced her husband Ahab to build a huge temple in Samaria to house great crowds of worshipers (2 Kings 10:21).

Groves, shrines, and temples of Baal and his consorts dotted the landscape, while Jezebel's prophets poisoned the minds of her people with lies and false teaching. One of their chief tenets was that Baal governed the waters and brought fertility to the soil and to the people. He was the god of rivers and rain and all other sources of water. A stele of Baal at the Louvre, in Paris, shows him standing on a subterranean river brandishing a mace and a spear, the end of which is tipped with vegetation, an allusion to his alleged ability to bring fertility to the land.

Baal, of course, was only an idol, a piece of rock with no power in it, but behind the idol skulked the devil and his minions (1 Corinthians 10:20), whose business it is to blight and ruin and bring sterility to everything that God has created and loves.

Elisha's business was to undo the effect of Satan's malicious and deadly influence and teach others how to undo it. He knew, and he wanted the young prophets to know, that their battle was "not against flesh and blood, but against the rulers, against the authorities, against the powers of this dark world and against the spiritual forces of evil in the heavenly realms" (Ephesians 6:12). If anything was to be done on earth, it must be done in the invisible realm of the Spirit. And so Elisha preached this simple, symbolic message.

He asked for a new bowl filled with salt, and he poured its contents into the mouth of the spring. The spring was instantly "healed." More telling was Elisha's brief explanation in verse 21: "This is what the Lord says: 'I have healed this water. Never again will it cause death or make the land unproductive.' "

The new jar represented the young prophet Elisha—a *parvenu*, an untested and unproven newcomer. It was an ordinary clay pot filled with salt, which, in those days, was a healing agent used to cleanse and disinfect.

And so two elements combine: a simple vessel pouring out salt, and God acting out of the invisible realm of the Spirit to heal the spring. *"I have healed this water,"* God said.

Paul put it this way: "We have this treasure [the Word of Christ] in jars of clay [our ordinary humanity] to show that the all-surpassing power is from God and not from us" (2 Corinthians 4:7).

God's Word, not our intellect, personality, training, experience, or clever presentation, is the power of the spoken word. Even Paul who was highly educated and intellectually gifted beyond most of his peers realized that the power of his preaching was God's power and not some acquired or innate ability of his own. "When I came to you, brothers," he wrote on one occasion, "I did not come with eloquence or superior wisdom as I proclaimed to you the testimony about God. . . . I came to you in weakness and fear, and with much trembling. My message and my preaching were not with wise and persuasive words, but with a demonstration of the Spirit's power" (1 Corinthians 2:1, 3–4).

This is a comforting thought to those of us who are not particularly articulate, gifted orators. We should labor, of course, to be clear and reasonable in our speaking; but the power of the Word does not lie in our ability to express it. It rests instead on the fact that when we speak God's Word, it is God Himself who is speaking. As Paul said in 1 Thessalonians 2:13: "We also thank God continually because, when you received the word of God, which you heard from us, you accepted it not as the word of men, but as it actually is, the word of God, which is at work in you who believe."

And when God speaks, mysterious, miraculous things begin to happen: Memories are cleansed, passions are purified, bitter hearts are sweetened, and souls are seasoned with beauty and grace. His Word, even spoken ineptly, will not return empty, but will accomplish what He desires and achieve the purpose for which He sends it.

So then, "Let your conversation [speech] be always full of grace, seasoned with salt" (Colossians 4:6). No other Word will do.[1]

> Oh what a mystery is shown
> When God makes sweet with salt my blunder
> Upon the earth where sin has sown
> Deceitful streams. His grace, my wonder.
>
> —JIM CATLIN

---

1. The author of 2 Kings adds this final note: "The water has remained wholesome to this day." The water at Jericho is still sweet or "healed." I know. I have tasted it.

BAD NEWS BEARS

If Love will not compel them to come in we must leave them to God who is the judge of all.

—JOHN WESLEY

2 Kings 2:23–24

Occasionally some friends and I fish a remote mountain stream west of our home in Boise that passes through an abandoned ranch and an ancient apple orchard. Rumor has it that a cranky, old bear hangs out there.

I've never seen him, but I always move my feet a little faster when I pass that way. As a friend of mine says, "A bear makes you think about things"—apropos of which is a story about Elisha and the two bears, a startling account that comes up for criticism now and then when God's ways are in question.

It appears from first reading that a group of small children tumbled out of the city of Bethel to poke innocent fun at Elisha's bald pate, and the prophet, in high dudgeon, set some angry bears on them. Canadian poet A. M. Klein refers to the

> Vengeance that bears
> Wreaked for the honour
> Of forty-two hairs!

No. Not for a minute. Here's what happened. Elisha was retracing his steps through the land he had traveled with his mentor, Elijah, reliving, perhaps, his memories of that association. As he made his way up the road that ascended the wadi from Jericho and through the dense forest that surrounded Bethel in those days, he was accosted by a band of hostile young men and women. These were not "little children," as some suppose; the word used to describe them is used of Solomon when he was twenty (1 Kings 3:7) and of David in a context in which he is described as "a brave man and a warrior" (1 Samuel 16:18). The term can refer to anyone up to age thirty.

Their taunt, "Go up," was a scoffing reference to the report of Elijah's translation to heaven and was similar in spirit to the mocking crowd at Jesus' feet: "Come down from the cross, if you are the Son of God!" (Matthew 27:40). And the epithet "Baldhead" was more insulting than it first appears. In the ancient Semitic world, it was a crude insult, perhaps because lepers shaved their heads.

This was not a crowd of playful children, but a gang of sullen, insolent men and women who had chosen evil and gathered to mock the God of Israel and His word. They were apostates who took delight in ridicule and contempt, hoping to prejudice others against Elisha's message. Their purpose was to run God's prophet out of town.

Bethel had long been a center of evil in Israel, one of the idol sites established by Jeroboam, the son of Nebat, who had "caused Israel to commit" sin (1 Kings 16:19). The city had been further degraded by Jezebel's Baal worship and the sensual rites of the Asherah. Hosea, in his day, dubbed the city Beth Aven, "House of Wickedness," for it was a representative city, symbolic of Israel's evil culture (Hosea 10:5).

The inhabitants of Bethel had last seen Elisha in company with Elijah, and the rumor of Elijah's translation to heaven and Elisha's investiture had reached them. They heard that Elisha, now shrouded in Elijah's mantle, was the old prophet's successor. So there was more at stake than the prophet's hair or lack thereof. This was a direct assault on God and His name and could deter those who might be struggling upward into the light. In their scoffing these young men were scorning God and His Word and leading others astray.

Contempt and ridicule of God's people, blasphemy, and denial of God's work—these are the weapons frequently employed by God's opponents. Scorn is the refuge of small minds, as they say, but it may triumph because it can wither weak souls and keep them from hearing what God in His mercy has to say.

So, the 2 Kings 2 text tells us, Elisha "looked at them"—a look as deep as the one our Lord cast on the rich young ruler—and then announced judgment, one with David in his imprecatory prayers (Psalm 139:19–22), and with Paul in his blunt anathema on those who would frustrate God's efforts to bring salvation to the world (1 Corinthians 16:22).[1] And "two bears came out of the woods and mauled forty-two of the youths."

Mauled is exactly right, for these young people were not killed, but "cut up," to stay with the precise meaning of the Hebrew word. God is ever the God of another chance. And then another.

Here I think of Felix, the Roman governor of Judea, before whom Paul appeared at Caesarea (Acts 23:23–24:27). Felix was a murderous, vicious tyrant on the order of Saddam Hussein, hated by Romans and Jews alike. He capriciously detained Paul for two years at Caesarea, or so it would seem capricious. In reality the apostle remained in prison because God wanted to give Felix and his wife Drusilla an opportunity to repent. Paul spoke to them of self-control (which Felix and Drusilla sorely lacked) and judgment that was surely coming.

---

1. We must distinguish between personal wrongs, which we must readily forgive, and deliberate attacks upon God and His work of salvation. Paul draws that distinction in his letter to his young friend Timothy: "Alexander the metalworker did me a great deal of harm. The Lord will repay him for what he has done. You too should be on your guard against him, because he strongly opposed our message" (2 Timothy 4:14–15). The "harm" Alexander did to Paul was not to his person but to his "message," and he was now engaged in stirring up opposition to Timothy's proclamation of the gospel. But then, as if to put in plain contrast the distinction between those who oppose God's work and those who wrong us, Paul follows with a personal word: "At my first defense, no one came to my support, but everyone deserted me." How cruel that Paul's converts would desert the elderly apostle in his hour of deep need. What shall be done to them? Surely they're worthy of Paul's anathema! Not so. "May it not be held against them" (2 Timothy 4:16).

Although Felix was "well acquainted with the Way," he would have none of it and eventually turned away.

What a waste, you may say; so much time and energy expended on "worthless" folks. Paul could have been evangelizing the world!

But Felix and Drusilla *were* Paul's world for that time, and they were not worthless. They were objects of God's love. God is a God of wisdom and grace, and He was not willing for them to perish. (You can read the story for yourself in Acts 24.)

But although judgment is delayed, it cannot be avoided. Felix's cruel suppression of Jewish rioters at Caesarea was the final straw for Nero, who was then the emperor; he sent Felix into exile and oblivion. Josephus says that Drusilla, his wife, the beautiful, proud daughter of Agrippa, whom Felix seduced away from her husband, died with their son during the volcanic eruption of Vesuvius in AD 79.

Judgment is God's "strange work," long deferred, for He does not want anyone to perish. But those who oppose the truth will not endure forever.

> *A little while*, and the wicked will be no more;
>   though you look for them, they will not be found
> (Psalm 37:10, italics mine).

As soon as a man or woman wants to make progress toward God and become useful for His purposes, the enemies of the faith will oppose him or her. You can count on it. But there's no need to be troubled. "Every plant that my heavenly Father has not planted will be pulled up by the roots," Jesus promised His disciples. "Leave them [alone]" (Matthew 15:13).

It's just a matter of time.

A FOOL'S ERRAND

Never underestimate the ingenuity
of complete fools.

—DOUGLAS ADAMS,
THE HITCHHIKER'S GUIDE
TO THE GALAXY

2 Kings 3:1–24

King Joram doesn't get much ink in the Bible, but what little is spilled on his behalf suggests that he, like his father Ahab, did things in the worst possible way, going about his business with an ice-cold logic that excluded God from his thinking. Therein lay his foolishness.

There was some decency in him, at least in the beginning: He "got rid of the sacred stone of Baal that his father [Ahab] had made." But he stubbornly "clung to the sins of Jeroboam the son of Nebat," placing his faith in idols and other material goods, going about his business with an ice-cold logic that excluded God from his thinking. Therein lies his, and our, foolishness.

His story begins with an ill-advised attempt to quell the rebellion of King Mesha of Moab who, upon Ahab's death, refused to give tribute to Israel. Joram was determined to make him pay.

Having mustered Israel's army, he went to elicit support from King Jehoshaphat of Judah, his neighbor to the south. Jehoshaphat responded with alacrity. "I will go with you," he said, the same answer he had given to Ahab some years before that had resulted in an alliance in which he had almost lost his life and for which he had been roundly rebuked by Jehu the seer: "Should you help the wicked and love those who hate the LORD?" (2 Chronicles 19:2). Then Jehoshaphat had allied himself with Ahab's evil son Ahaziah to reconstruct Solomon's vast navy, a sublime madness that had resulted in a second scolding: "Because you have made an alliance with Ahaziah, the LORD will destroy what you have made." Indeed, his "ships were wrecked" (2 Chronicles 20:37) (all of which proves the mule skinner's adage that you never learn anything the second time you get kicked by a mule). Now he was about to become a three-time loser.

So, to move on with the story, the kings, committed to their folly, formed their plan: "By what route shall we attack?" King Joram asked his ally.

There were two possible routes into Moab, east of the Dead Sea: One could attack from the north or take a more circuitous route, south around the Dead Sea. The northern route was shorter, but better defended. Furthermore, an assault from the north meant moving the armies across a deep gorge formed by the Arnon River, three miles wide and 2,300 feet deep, the Near Eastern equivalent of the Grand Canyon. The southern route was much longer, but less likely to be defended. Jehoshaphat's advice was to go south, through the desert of Edom. No one took counsel from the Lord.

The devil is in the details, as they say. The kings, now including the king of Edom, vastly underestimated the difficulties of the desert. After seven days of marching and having reached the southern end of the Dead Sea, the army ran out of food and water.

In the meantime the Moabites, having discerned Jehoshaphat's strategy, moved their army to the south. "Every man, young and old, who could bear arms was called up and stationed on the border" (2 Kings 3:21). Confronted with armed-to-the-teeth guerillas swarming the thickets around them, and unable to retreat into the wilderness, the kings found themselves in desperate trouble.

Joram exclaimed, "Has the Lord called us together only to hand us over to Moab?" ignoring the fact that the Lord had not called them to do anything. It was the kings' business from beginning to end, which manifests the extent to which we, like these men, in our own foolishness, leave God out of our decisions, dig ourselves into deep holes, and in our despair or stubborn defiance keep on digging.

However, even the worst fools are a little wise. Jehoshaphat resorted at last to the Lord: "Is there no prophet of the LORD here, that we may inquire of the LORD through him?" When told that Elisha was in their midst, Jehoshaphat sighed with remembrance: "The word of the LORD is with him."[1]

Then the three kings, of Israel, Judah, and Edom, "went down" to Elisha, a description dealing with more than the slope of the ground, for God could do nothing for these men until they came down from their pedestals of self-reliance and pride.

When the kings arrived, the prophet gave in to their entreaty, for despite Joram's indifference to spiritual things, Jehoshaphat was God's child. So Elisha called for a musician,[2] and while the music was playing, the word of the Lord came to Elisha: "Make this valley full of ditches. For this is what the LORD says: You will see neither wind nor rain, yet this valley will be filled with water, and you, your cattle and your other animals will drink."

As directed, the soldiers dug pits along the sides of the wadi on which they were stranded. The next morning, about the time for offering the evening sacrifice in Jerusalem,[3] the wadi began to fill with water, though there was no sign of wind or rain. A sudden storm had burst on the mountains to the southeast and sent a rush of water

---

1. Elisha had marched with the armies but had held his peace as the disaster unfolded. He knew that sometimes a good scare can do more good than good counsel.

2. Good music is God reaching out to touch us. Music is less affected by the Fall, I think, than other aspects of creation—some of it, that is. It has power to bring peace. Perhaps we're surprised by its joy or by the touch of harmony we have lost in the Fall, which is why we don't like dissonance. Yes, music is God reaching out to touch us— like a sunset.

3. Events in Israel's history were often correlated with events taking place in the Jerusalem temple. That's because everything centers on God's salvation. The flow of grace came when the lamb was sacrificed, a symbol of that day when the Lamb of God would be sacrificed and take away our sin. God's grace is not based on mercy, but on the Cross and a finished salvation.

down the valley, filling the pits and disappearing as suddenly as it had come. God's grace had been poured out on the armies.

When the Moabites looked across the valley that morning, the sun was shining on the pools. The soil in that part of the world tints water blood-red, and the rising sun shining on the trenches enhanced the illusion. "That's blood!" the Moabites said, thinking that Israel and her allies had fought and slaughtered one another. "Now to the plunder," they shouted. But when the Moabites came to the camp of Israel, the Israelites rose up and fought them until they fled. Thus Israel's armies were spared from destruction, and the Moabites were put to flight.

I'm reminded in all this that we, like these two kings, play the fool; we make decisions on our own and apart from God, heedless choices that ruin our businesses, impair our reputations, and imperil our homes. We humiliate and shame ourselves.

Our humiliation, however, can be the beginning of our salvation if it leads us to humility, for this is the key that opens God's heart. He has said,

> This is the one I esteem:
> > he who is humble and contrite in spirit,
> > and trembles at my word (Isaiah 66:2).

When we return to Him, He fills our lives with His love. We may have to live with the results of our folly, but we have the full assurance of renewed fellowship with Him. God resists the proud, but He cannot resist the humble. He favors them and showers them with grace.

Humiliation and shame bring us to God for His love and acceptance. When we have fallen, we fall into His hands.

WINS AND LOSSES

He tackled the thing that couldn't be done!
With a will he went right to it.
He tackled the thing that couldn't be done—
And he couldn't do it.

—AUTHOR UNKNOWN

2 Kings 3:25–27

WARM-UP

In the mid-1800s an Anglican medical missionary, F. A. Klein, traveling east of the Jordan, came across a black, basalt stone containing a lengthy inscription. Klein copied a few words and then reported his find to the German consul who began negotiations to move the stone to the Berlin Museum.

Some Arabs, sensing the value of the stone, built a fire under it, threw cold water on it, and broke it into small pieces that they planned to sell separately. Eventually most of the fragments were found, and the text was reconstructed. Out of 1,100 lines, 669 were recovered.

The inscription refers to the triumph of "Mesha, son of Chemosh," the Mesha mentioned in the 2 Kings biblical text. On the stone King Mesha tells the world how he threw off the yoke of Yahweh's people and by so doing honored his god Chemosh. "[Israel's king] said, 'I will oppress Moab.' In my days he spoke thus, but I have triumphed over him [Ahab] and his house [Ahaziah and Joram] and Israel utterly perished forever."

It happened this way: After the initial rout of Mesha's army (2 Kings 3:21–24), Israel's forces fought their way northward through the land of Moab, pulling down the walls of every city until they came to Kir Hareseth, the northern capital of Moab. Here their advance ground to a halt.

Kir Hareseth was built on a rocky hill that rises three thousand feet above sea level, surrounded on three sides by steep valleys, twelve- to fifteen-hundred feet deep, topped with impenetrable walls. Israel could not break through. All they could do was post sharpshooters on the heights to harass defenders and mount a prolonged siege.

At one point, "the king of Moab took with him seven hundred swordsmen to break through to the king of Edom." Perhaps he thought the Edomites were the weakest link in the Israeli alliance or that they would fight with less resolve because they were conscripts. As the biblical author puts it in his characteristic laconic way, the Moabites "failed."

In desperation, the Moabite king "took his firstborn son, who was to succeed him as king, and offered him as a sacrifice on the city wall." With this horrifying act, Mesha turned defeat into victory. Israel's army retreated in disarray, and Moab was free from Israel's yoke for the next two hundred years. In that sense, "Israel utterly perished forever."

A recent find throws light on this event. In 1987 a cuneiform tablet from Ugarit was published, the text suggesting that Mesha was following the rules of Canaanite "holy war": When an enemy attacks a city, the people should pray to Baal for victory. Baal will hear that prayer if it is supplemented by the sacrifice of a firstborn. Then "[Baal] shall drive the force from your gates."[1]

The text itself is dated about 1200 BC, four centuries before Mesha, but the practice has been documented as late as the Roman period. Diodorus of Sicily (c. 50 BC) wrote that when the Roman armies were besieging Carthage, the Carthaginians "selected two hundred of the noblest children and sacrificed them publicly."

---

1. Information and quotes from Baruch Margalit, *Biblical Archaeology Review,* November–December 1986, p. 63. Margalit notes: "The author of the Ugaritic text apparently anticipated this reaction of mass hysteria when he confidently predicted the withdrawal of the attacking force. . . . It follows that Mesha's sacrifice of his son, rather than unprecedented, was in fact an integral, if seldom implemented, part of an age-old Canaanite tradition of sacral warfare."

This sacrificial practice is also mentioned by Eusebius, the church historian, who claims that he heard of it from the Phoenician historian Sanchuniaton. According to this tradition, when Canaanite cities were under siege, it was their practice to "sacrifice their beloved children."

The author of the Canaanite text cited above confidently predicted the withdrawal of attacking forces after a human sacrifice. On the occasion of Mesha's cruel act, it worked. The horrible, sickening spectacle stunned the armies of Israel into submission. They shrank in horror from the walls of the city. Thus ended the campaign against Moab.

In 2 Kings Israel's historian notes that God's army was demoralized because "great fury" came upon them. Some say the Moabites were emboldened by Mesha's sacrifice and broke through Israel's siege, in which case the "fury against Israel," would be a furious counterattack. Others suggest that the "fury" was God's wrath against Israel because of her national sin.

But there is another, simpler explanation, I believe. The word translated "fury" or "wrath" means "to break into pieces" (its noun form means "fragments" or "shards") and can denote a psychological breakdown. In other words, Israel "fell apart." Her warriors were emotionally shattered by the sacrifice of the king's son and so dispirited by the horrific event that they could fight no longer and broke off the siege. Thus Chemosh, Moab's Baal, was credited with the victory, and Yahweh, Israel's God, was humbled. The Moabite stone reports the result of the battle as such, and it stands today in the Louvre in Paris, a monument to Israel's bitter defeat.

Psalm 44 may have been written after this defeat by Moab. Israel's poet begins by praising God for past victories, wrought not by sword or human strength, but by God's hand "and the light of [God's] face, for [God] loved them." But then the psalm turns and talks of defeat, how the army was routed, slaughtered or scattered, disgraced, and humiliated. Finally the psalm ends with a prayer,

Rise up and help us;
  redeem us because of your unfailing love.

The apostle Paul well understood the message of Psalm 44. In Romans 8:35–37 he assures us that despite our defeats, nothing can separate us from the love of Christ, not "trouble or hardship or persecution or famine or nakedness or danger or sword." After saying this, Paul quotes Psalm 44:22:

For your sake we face death all day long,
  we are considered as sheep to be slaughtered.

Adversity is our lot, Paul notes. Yet "we are more than conquerors through him who loved us." We will taste defeat from time to time, but even so, we are loved with everlasting love.

There are days when we too falter. Our best foot forward is a bitter embarrassment; our best efforts go belly-up. We get discouraged and despondent; we shrink from further endeavor; we think of quitting, and sometimes we do. We are, after all, failed, flawed creatures, plagued by human inadequacy and inconsistency. The spirit may be willing, but the flesh is weak, and we will suffer humiliating defeat from time to time.

Nevertheless, we must never give up. We must press on, through the ups and downs of life, through its wins and losses. God is not ashamed to call us His brothers and coworkers, and He will never stop giving us work to do. We are His, for better or worse. He could certainly do better; He could hardly do worse. But He has chosen us. He has not chosen angels to do His holy work. He has chosen us, frail and failed human beings. He has much more for us to do.

Let's get on with it!

BEHIND CLOSED DOORS

"What should I do then, mem?"
"Go your way, laddie . . . and say your prayers."

—GEORGE MACDONALD, *THE FISHERMAN'S LADY*

2 Kings 4:1–7

Josephus, the Jewish historian, suggests that the woman in the story was the wife of Obadiah, that good man who provided food and shelter for the persecuted prophets during Ahab and Jezebel's reign (1 Kings 18:4) and thus, according to Josephus, impoverished himself. This may be, but we'll never know for sure. The biblical text simply describes her as "a wife of a man from the company of the prophets," one anonymous, unremarkable woman who became the victim of circumstances beyond her control.

The woman's story is one of accumulated grief: Her husband died and left her destitute and deeply in debt; then her creditors came knocking at her door, demanding that she pay up or sell her two sons into slavery to compensate them.

Immediately, and with sound wisdom, she went to Elisha, the embodiment of God's presence in the land. She cried out, "Your servant my husband is dead, and you know that he revered the LORD. But now his creditor is coming to take my two boys as his slaves." Her words are a reminder that even those who "fear the Lord" may find themselves in deep trouble.

When Elisha heard the woman's plea, he didn't rush to meet her need, as we're inclined to do. Had he done so, she might have gained a little comfort, but not from the highest source, and she would have gained it too soon for her own good. No, instead Elisha asked the woman what she had at hand. "Nothing," she said, "except a little oil."

His response? "Go around and ask your neighbors for empty jars. Don't ask for just a few. Then go inside and shut the door behind you and your sons. Pour oil into all the jars, and as each is filled, put it to one side."

When I first read the prophet's words, I thought of Jesus' words, "When you pray, go into your room [in the interior of the house], *close the door* and pray to your Father, who is unseen. Then your Father, who sees what is done in secret, will reward you" (Matthew 6:6, italics mine). Nothing is said about prayer in the Old Testament account, but it's significant to me that Jesus' phrase, translated "close the door," corresponds roughly to the Greek translation of this Old Testament text, which Jesus Himself read and frequently quoted.[1] Could it be that He had this story in mind?

If so, I suggest that prayer is a matter of shutting ourselves away from all other dependencies—from background, experience, training, and past accomplishments, from all the props of reason and intellect, closing everything and everyone out, and closeting ourselves with God alone (see also 2 Kings 4:33). We detach ourselves from all outward things and attach ourselves inwardly to the Lord alone. This is where God works His wonders.

So, as the story goes, Elisha directed the widow to "shut the door behind her and her sons. They brought the jars to her and she kept pouring. When the jars were full, she said to her son, 'Bring me another one.'

"But he replied, 'There is not a jar left.' Then the oil stopped flowing." Then the widow sold the oil, paid off her debts, and lived on what remained.

---

1. The only difference is that the Greek translation of 2 Kings 4:4 uses an intensified form of the verb and puts it in the future tense: *apokleiseis tân thuran* (you shall shut the door *tight!*). Jesus uses the simple form of the same verb and states the action as participle, *kleisas tân thuran* (having shut the door).

The widow's needs were met, but something more important occurred: She learned to carry *everything* to God in prayer, or so I believe.

It seems that the early church asked its senior members to take on a particular ministry of love and prayer. This has now become my special work. I grieve with a friend over a prodigal son and can think of nothing hopeful to say. And so I pray. I listen to a pastor whose heart is broken by criticism and disapproval, and I can do nothing to change others' perceptions of him and his ministry. And so I pray. I stand by the bed of a desperately ill child, and I have no power to heal. And so I pray.

I pray, but, more important, by my praying I teach *others* to pray. I may not be able to bring help to those in deep and desperate need, but I can encourage them to bring every need to the One who gives "grace to help in time of need" (Hebrews 4:16). This is my deepest joy. Elisha could have met this woman's dearth by giving her a gift of money or gathering food from her friends, but he gave her a greater gift—the gift of a lifetime: He taught *her* to pray.

A SAFE PLACE

Frodo was now safe. . . . The house was, as Bilbo had long ago reported, "a perfect house, whether you like food or sleep or story telling or singing, or just sitting and thinking best, or a pleasant mixture of them all." Merely to be there was a cure for weariness, fear and sadness.

—J. R. R. TOLKIEN

2 Kings 4:8–10

Elisha was making his way through the villages of Israel and came to Shunem, a town on the flanks of Little Mount Hermon near Joram's summer palace at Jezreel. Despite Shunem's proximity to the corrupt court, however, there was another spirit in Shunem, for Elisha was welcome there and frequently ministered on the Sabbath and on other occasions (see 2 Kings 4:23).

Hospitality was always extended—that was the custom among God's people—and it seems that a certain "well-to-do woman" (the adjective suggests nobility and is reminiscent of the "noble woman" of Proverbs 31) was particularly insistent that Elisha stay with her and her husband in their home. It seems Elisha was reluctant at first, but finally he yielded to her urging and found the home a pleasant place of refreshment and recreation.

One day the woman said to her husband, "I know that this man who often comes our way is a holy man of God. Let's make a small room on the roof and put in it a bed and a table, a chair and a lamp for him. Then he can stay there whenever he comes to us." The Shunammite called the man of God "holy"—a measure of the work God was doing to modify Elisha. During his visits she had opportunities to observe him in unguarded moments, and she saw that he rang true. Would that all of us had that reputation.

At some point the woman suggested to her husband that he build a chamber on their roof where the prophet could stay whenever he visited. It seems a modest proposal, yet it implies giving up the most cherished part of an Israelite home, for the roof was the place where families and friends gathered under a canopy for meals and conversation and to find relief from heat that built up in the house during the day. This was no small act of self-sacrifice and service.

In Palestine an outside stair led to the roof; it was not necessary to pass through the interior of the building to get there, which meant that Elisha had unrestricted access and egress, privacy and a place of restful seclusion.

The four pieces of furniture provided by the host were the essentials of that time—a bed, a table, a lamp, and a chair. But there's something special about the chair. Everywhere else in the Old Testament (1 Kings 10:9; 22:10, 19; Psalm 122:5), the word means "a seat of honor," sometimes translated as "throne." (A leather recliner comes to mind.) The point seems to be that the woman and her husband spared no effort to provide a warm, comfortable setting for the prophet. Later in the story (v. 13) Elisha commented, "You have taken all this trouble for us," "trouble" suggesting a good deal of hustle and bustle. The Greek Septuagint translates with a word that means to "stand outside oneself," or, as we would say, to out-do oneself.

Here is a reminder to be hospitable to those who pass by. Hospitality seems a small thing, the activity of those who have nothing better to do, but God's Word speaks to the contrary.

Peter, for example, points out that life is short, so we should give ourselves to things that count—prayer, love, and hospitality, to name the first three (1 Peter 4:7–11). Here is an inspired answer to the old question, "What would I do if I knew that I would die today?" Peter's answer: nothing out of the ordinary; just what I should be doing every other day of my life, loving and serving those in need. And, according to Peter, one of the ways I can serve the needy is through hospitality. Paul puts it plainly: "Share with God's people who are in need. Practice hospitality" (Romans 12:13).

One Greek word for loving others is *philadelphia,* meaning "loving brothers." The word for hospitality in the New Testament is *philoxenia,* meaning "loving outsiders." Hospitality is more than entertaining family and friends; it is reaching out beyond our comfort zone to strangers.

In the ancient world hospitality was especially needed, because inns were dark, dangerous hovels. Things are different today—clean, safe hotels and motels abound. But the principle remains the same. Hospitality means reaching out to those in need with kindness, generosity, and comfort. It may mean providing bed and breakfast or a place for an extended stay. (There's an unchanging, essential element to the widow's furnishings: a bed, a table, a chair, and a lamp.) We can house visiting missionaries and speakers, foreign exchange students, unwed mothers, and battered women. We can open our homes for Bible studies and youth gatherings.

But hospitality entails more than opening our homes. It means opening our hearts as well. Beyond housing others, hospitality means being *ourselves* a safe place for strangers—a center of peace, a haven in our madcap world where the harried and weary can rest in our presence. It means providing a sheltering environment for others at home or away.

I like the word-picture painted by Hermes, a second-century Christian. Those who open their hearts to others, he says, are "trees that overshadow the sheep." I ask myself, *How can I become a tree?* It's an attitude that grows in me, I think, as I reflect on God's eagerness to take me in and shelter me.

PROCREATION

A wondrous son she did embrace,
Heaven's handiwork, and special grace.

—BENJAMIN COLMAN

2 Kings 4:12–17

Elisha asked the Shunammite woman, "What can I do for you?" "I have a home among my own people," she replied, an idiom that suggests quiet contentment.

But Gehazi, Elisha's servant, detected a deep sorrow she was unwilling to share. "She has no son," he observed, "and her husband is old."

Childlessness was a cause for deep regret and social reproach in the ancient world. Jacob's wife Rachel, speaking for many childless couples, even now, cried out: "Give me children, or I'll die!" (Genesis 30:1).

The same sentiment occurs in a Canaanite poem from the fourteenth century BC titled "The Legend of Aqhat." A hero-ruler named Dan-el is forlorn because he has no offspring. Dan-el then plies Baal with food and wine until Baal appeals to his father-god, El:

> May you bless him,
> O Bull, El, my father.
> Beautify him O creator of creatures,
> So shall there be a son in his house;
> a scion in the midst of his palace.

It is not El, however, that beautifies couples with offspring, but Yahweh, Israel's God, who, in common grace, creates life in the womb. It is God's nature to pour out blessings, even on those who do not acknowledge His love.

Elisha, being a prophet and understanding God's intentions, promised the Shunammite woman that she would hold a child in her arms, "about this season, according to the time of life," as the King James Version says. The text is difficult and has mystified many, but it suggests that the miracle consisted of a normal sequence of conception according to the woman's cycle and nine-month gestation; the process appeared normal in every way. This reminds me that every delivery is a miracle, even those for which we think that everything depends upon us. Though a natural process appears to be at work, it is God who forms the fetus in the womb (note Isaiah 49:5; Jeremiah 1:5).

Ever since I first read G. K. Chesterton's *Orthodoxy*, I have been intrigued by his idea that God is still creating the world and everything in it. He proposed that just as a child delights in seeing a thing done again and again, God delights in the repetition and "monotony" of creation every day. "It is possible that God says every morning, 'Do it again' to the sun; and every evening, 'Do it again' to the moon. It may not be automatic necessity that makes all daisies alike; it may be that God makes every daisy separately, but has never got tired of making them. . . . The repetition in Nature may not be a mere recurrence; it may be a theatrical ENCORE!" It is possible that every new emergence—every blade of grass, every butterfly, every billowing cloud—is a new and special creation invented out of God's wisdom, excitement, and artistry. He paints each pansy as it emerges in the spring. He colors every leaf in the fall. He ponders every act of creation, shouts "encore!" and the whole business begins all over again, the business of creation that began "in the beginning" and is still going on to this day.

Thus, by analogy, every human conception is a creation. God says, "Let us make humankind in our image, according to our likeness"— and human life springs into being! We think of the process as purely natural; we conceive a child, and it grows to term on its own. In truth it is preternatural—*a miraculous creation*. (It occurs to me at the same time that any given conception might be God's final creation, in which case the human race would very soon be extinct, for our existence, despite our heroic efforts to perpetuate ourselves, is solely dependent on God's creative handiwork.)

Chesterton suggested the idea of ongoing creation to me, but David, Israel's poet, convinced me, for he describes God first "musing" and then "weaving" David together in the darkness of his mother's womb. He did so, David insists, "before one of them [the various elements that became 'David'] came to be [were in existence]" (Psalm 139:13–16). The Hebrew text for verse 16 reads: "Your eyes saw my unformed substance and in Your book they [David's 'component parts'] were written day by day before there was one of them." The metaphor is that of a "journal" in which God wrote His ideas of what David would become and then brought each idea into being through His handiwork in the womb.

In other words, God created David out of nothing—no, out of Himself. He imagined the person who was to be and then brought that person into being according to a preimagined plan.

Put another way, we begin as a gleam in our heavenly Father's eye and are shaped by Love into a unique, immediate creation— immediate in the ordinary sense of "unmediated," in that we come directly from the inventive heart and hand of God.

That means that I am special and so are you—and so is everyone else in the world. This being true, I must be prolife in the purest sense of the word in that I sanctify *all* human life[1]—Stanford University sophisticates and untutored semi-illiterates, Seattle socialites and skid-row derelicts, winsome children and doddering curmudgeons, fundamentalist preachers and left-wing political pundits, Muslims and Christians, homosexuals and heterosexuals, antiabortion enthusiasts and prochoice activists. Every person—of any class, age, sex, and race—is a unique production of our Creator's genius.

Which is why Jesus said we should never call anyone a "fool."[2]

---

1. The Bible supports the sanctity of human life and not life in general, for human beings alone are created in the image and likeness of God, that is, more like God than any other creature.

2. Matthew 5:22. His word here, *hracá*, means "worthless."

SEVEN SNEEZES

Not long embraced, but on her knees
Arrested by a fierce disease,
Scarce could he cry, My Head, My Head!
E'er the dear parent saw him dead:
She laid him breathless on the bed.
   Deep was her anguish, yet her peace
She held, and went to God for ease.

—BENJAMIN COLMAN

2 Kings 4:18-37

Years passed, during which the Shunammite's miracle child grew through the stages of Israelite childhood: from yeled (newborn) to yonek (nursing baby) to olel (nursing child who eats baby food) to gamel (weaned child) to taph (one who clings to mother's apron) to elem (one who is strong and able to work in the fields).

One day the boy was working beside his father, when the boy cried out and collapsed. A servant carried him to his mother, who held him on her lap and rocked him until he died.

She carried the body up to Elisha's rooftop chamber, laid it on Elisha's bed, saddled a donkey, and went to hunt down the prophet. Once she found him, she poured out her distress: "Did I ask you for a son, my lord? Didn't I tell you, 'Don't raise my hopes'?" Elisha had broken the heart he had hoped to heal.

Elisha immediately sent Gehazi with his staff posthaste to Shunem with instructions to lay it on the child's face. Gehazi did as he was told, but there was "no sound or response." He failed, and Elisha knew he would fail, for there is no magic or medicine that will stave off death. Only "the LORD . . . makes alive" (1 Samuel 2:6).

The narrative passes over Elisha's long journey from Carmel to Shunem, but it must have been dark when Elisha and the mother arrived back at her home. Elisha mounted the stairs, went into his room, "shut the door on the two of them [the child and the prophet], and prayed to the LORD."

"Now the prophet is at his work in right earnest," Spurgeon wrote, "and we have a noble opportunity of learning from him the secret of raising children from the dead."

Then Elisha stretched himself out on the lifeless body as Elijah had once (1 Kings 17), "mouth to mouth, eyes to eyes, hands to hands," and the boy's body began to warm. Elisha then paced the floor and waited and stretched himself again on the child's body. The child sneezed seven times (an onomatopoetic *atishah,* in Hebrew), an indication that respiration and life had returned. Then the boy opened his eyes.

Elisha called the Shunammite mother and placed her son in her arms. She could only bow in humble thanks, one of those who by faith "received back their dead, raised to life again" (Hebrews 11:35).

Not all of us will "receive back" our dead, at least not in this life. They will not come to us; we will go to them, as David, mourning an infant son, noted in 2 Samuel 12:23. We await heaven and its cure for all childhood diseases and death. In the meantime we have our Father's comfort and grace.

> Mind, gracious friend, the word she said,
> *All well*, and yet the child was dead.
> What God ordains is well and best.
> Well 'tis with ours, when gone to rest.
> It's well with us, who stay behind,
> If more from earth and sense refined
> We're patient, prayerful, meek, resigned.
>
> —BENJAMIN COLMAN

Ah, but there may be harder things to bear and harder still to comfort, even for God Himself. Time may heal a heart broken by the death of a child, but there are feelings that time may not numb. Can we easily forget the child who is dead in trespasses and sins, where "there is no sound" or sign of life, and nothing we say or do can save? Can anything assuage the gnawing agony of that loss? Elisha supplies a way.

We can enter into our room and "shut the door." We can pray. "One thing is clear with regard to every trouble," George MacDonald said. "The natural way with it is straight to the Father's knee." We can closet ourselves with God and bring into that place the imagined presence of the one we love. We may not know how to pray as we should, but we can "cry out in the night" and "lift up our hands for the lives of our young children" (see Lamentations 2:19). We can dwell on the name of the child and leave the difficulty with God.

We can love *fervently* (1 Peter 1:22 KJV), which in the Greek means "stretched out." Elisha "lay upon the boy," stretched himself out. We, in like manner, can warm our children with mercy and compassion and stretch ourselves out in love. Love and compassion penetrate the heart that has been hardened by words.

And we can love *again*. Elisha did not give up; he attempted to resuscitate the boy a second time. So we too must never give up. God is at work through our prayers and love, though we may not see immediate signs of life. We are in the middle of the story; there's more to it than we can know.

A FAMINE IN THE LAND

Knowledge is a deadly friend
When no one sets the rules.

—KING CRIMSON,
"21ST-CENTURY SCHIZOID MAN"

2 Kings 4:38–44

There was famine in the land, a dearth that underscored a more serious famine—

not a famine of food or a thirst for water,
but a famine of hearing the words of the LORD (Amos 8:11).

Few were willing to hear what the Lord had to say.

Here and there, however, were enclaves of God-fearing Israelites, men and women who had not bowed to Baal, who hungered and thirsted for righteousness. They were represented in part by the young prophets at Gilgal who sat at Elisha's feet.

Man does not live by bread alone, it's said, but he does live by bread. Knowing that hungry men must be fed, Elisha dispatched his servant Gehazi to prepare a hearty meal. Gehazi, in turn, sent one of the students off to gather wild herbs to put in the stew.

The young man went into the field and filled his tunic with edible plants; he included gourds from a wild vine unfamiliar to him, thinking, perhaps, to add spice to the stew. But the vine was poisonous. Unfortunately he shredded all he had gathered into one container and mixed it together so that it was impossible to distinguish one ingredient from the other.

Gehazi, not realizing what the young man had done, prepared the dish and ladled it out for the group. Fortunately someone tasted danger and cried out to "the man of God," Elisha, "There is death in the pot!"

In my circles those who criticize camp cooks have to cook the next couple of meals, but Elisha had a better idea: He used the opportunity to teach his young men. He asked for a handful of meal, which he threw into the stew, and, as the author puts it laconically, "There was nothing harmful in the pot"—literally "not an evil 'word' " in the pot.

In *Bible History: Old Testament*, Alfred Edersheim notes, "the symbolic meaning of casting 'meal' into the pot." The agent of meal, an "ordinary and healthy food," was used to change "that which had been bitter and dangerous . . . into a palatable and nourishing diet." God performed a miracle through "the man of God," and this also has a "symbolic significance; the more so, that the 'sons of the prophets' had, as disciples, been learning from Elisha." In other words, the medium (the miracle) was the message, and the message was crystal clear: There is a healthy corrective to evil.

The story, as I see it, represents our everyday efforts to search our "field" of inquiry to gather facts to feed our minds. The field is the world, a world in which we're bombarded with information from all corners of the globe.

Facts stream at us through every medium like items on a swiftly moving conveyer belt, the validity and value of which we must quickly assess, a process Alvin Toffler calls "decisional speedup."[1]

One example of this phenomenon is MTV and other pop media. Images rush at us in a 24/7, kaleidoscopic catena: "reality" shows, mock-romantic dating scenarios, pseudo-documentaries, fast-moving, fragmented music videos, all vie for our attention and all are reinforced with cutting-edge technology that relentlessly assaults our visual and auditory senses.

---

1. I'm reminded here of the old "I Love Lucy" show and that oft-repeated, hilarious sketch with Lucy and Ethel in the candy factory.

There is little time to evaluate or make moral judgments. Good and evil are mixed together in a subtle brew, resulting in a strange new world in which contradiction, perplexity, and ambiguity prevail. This is our "postmodern" world, as we have come to characterize it, a world that alters its morality at will. Can we be certain of anything, or must we simply "pick and choose" right and wrong?

Many years ago I saw a cartoon depicting two people discussing good and evil. One said to the other, "I believe in evil. I just don't know what qualifies." This is our world today: one that does not know where the parameters are, an agnosticism that makes for a very dark and dangerous world.

We are like children in this regard: We long for the safety of a moral framework. It's unnatural to exist without benchmarks and reference points, and unnerving, like the sensations of an orbiting, weightless astronaut. Give me a sign, a word, that says, "This is up," or, "This is down."

Where is that fixed, enduring rule to which I can defer? Where are truths that transcend time, culture, and circumstance?

Norman Maclean raises that question in his autobiographical novella *A River Runs Through It*. It's a story about fly-fishing and a family's heartache over a free-spirited son, Paul, who drinks too much, lives too fast, and eventually dies in a back-alley brawl. But it's more than that: It's about a father's efforts to pass on to his two sons the underlying, unchanging values of his life. Most of the lessons are taught streamside. Maclean recalls one exchange with his father:

"What have you been reading?" I asked. "A book," he said. . . . "A good book."

Then he told me, "In the part I was reading it says the Word was in the beginning, and that's right. I used to think water was first, but if you listen carefully you will hear the words are underneath the water."

"That's because you're a preacher first and then a fisherman," I told him. "If you ask Paul, he will tell you that the words are formed out of water."

"No," my father said. "You are not listening carefully. The water runs over the words. . . ."

I looked to see where the book was left open and knew just enough Greek to recognize *logos* as the Word. I guessed from it and the argument that I was looking at the first verse of John.

Maclean concludes the novella: "The river was cut by the world's great flood and runs over rocks from the basement of time. . . . Under the rocks are the words. . . ."

"In the beginning was the Word," wrote John—a Word that is older than the rocks, a Word that is older than time, a Word that counteracts the effects of the toxins that pollute and perplex our minds these days.

We never get so progressive in our thinking that we can leave that Word behind. We must not "run ahead," as John wrote (2 John 9); we must go back—back to the prophets, back to Jesus and the apostles.

John was inveighing against avante garde thinkers, progressives who were looking for something new. But, as John insists, we must go back—back to the Word, which was from the beginning, back to the prophets and their revelations, back to Jesus and what apostles heard and saw, back to the truth "once for all entrusted" to God's children (Jude 3).

The only way out of the darkness of these days is a dash of meal, that fundamental health-giving food that is the Word of God, the only antidote for all that is not of God and thus is deadly. This is where we find reality and the knowledge of good and evil, and the ability to make our way through our dark and dangerous world with wisdom and safety.

"Dear ones, do not believe every spirit, but test the spirits [by God's Word] to see whether they are from God" (1 John 4:1).

MORE THAN ENOUGH

Though scarce enough for one it seemed,
He blessed and made it more.

—ANNIE JOHNSON FLINT

2 Kings 4:42–44

A man came from Baal–Shalisha, a region in Ephraim known as Shalisha in better times. With the advent of Jezebel's Baalism, the name of the region had been changed to Baal-Shalisha to reflect devotion to her god. But Jezebel's god was a figment god, as all "other gods" are figments of our imagination.[1]

To be sure, there are real forces behind every god, creating the illusion that they exist; but there are no other gods, only demons (1 Corinthians 8:4–6; 10:20), and demons cannot create good. They can only blight and ruin the good things God has created. "No one is good—except God alone," Jesus said (Luke 18:19).

This man, knowing that God, not Baal, had enriched his harvest, brought his offering, the firstfruits of his fields,[2] to the prophet Elisha, for there were no priests or Levites in Israel in those days. (All had fled to Judah to escape Jezebel's insane rage.) This was a gift for Elisha's sole good, enough to sustain him for a long time.

---

1. Baal was called *ben dagan* ("the son of grain") and *zebel ba'al arts* ("the prince the lord of the earth").

2. The "firstfruit" was the tithe set aside for the priests and Levites in Israel (Numbers 18:13; Deuteronomy 18:4). The priests in Israel had no "inheritance" (land), because they had been called to care for other people's souls and had no time to work their farms. Thus they were supported by the people to whom they ministered.

Here is an unexpected gift in a time of dire need. Elisha, like others, was hard pressed by the drought, but in the same spirit as the man who brought the gift, he determined to share it with his friends.

Elisha's attendant (probably Gehazi) pointed out the impracticality of giving the food away; there wasn't enough to go around, he argued. The gift might supply the wants of the prophet for a long time, but to set it before "a hundred men" (a round number for the community of prophets and their families) was to lose any good from the gift.

Elisha, however, issued a command to get on with the feeding, but more. . . . He added a promise that this scanty provision would be more than enough: "For this is what the LORD says: 'They will eat and have some left over.' " The verb translated "have some left over" literally means "to have more than enough."[3]

True to the prophet's word, when his servant set the meal before the people, "they ate and had some left over." There was more than enough for their needs.

I can't help but think of that occasion on which Jesus and His disciples were crossing the Sea of Galilee in their little boat and it occurred to them that they had no bread (Mark 8:14–21). Jesus had just fed the four thousand people with seven loaves of bread with seven full *baskets* left over! But they had forgotten to bring any of the bread that remained.

Jesus, aware of their discussion, asked them: "Don't you remember? When I broke the five loaves for the five thousand, how many basketfuls of pieces did you pick up?"

"Twelve," they replied.

"And when I broke the seven loaves for the four thousand, how many basketfuls of pieces did you pick up?"

---

3. The same verb in the same form occurs in Exodus 36:7, where Moses insisted that the people no longer bring their gifts to the artisans who were building the tabernacle because, as he put it, there was more than enough to finish the work. On two occasions, recorded in Matthew 14:13–21 and 15:32–39, our Lord fed a large crowd. Both times there was "more than enough."

They answered, "Seven."

He said to them, "Do you still not understand?" There is enough and more than enough.

Paul insists, "My God will meet all your needs according to his glorious riches in Christ Jesus" (Philippians 4:19). What a source: *God*. What a resource: *His riches*. His love is limitless; His supply is infinite. There is enough and "more than enough."

- Enough to exist gracefully with an ailing body or a failing mind.
- Enough to live with an irascible aging parent, a cantankerous husband, a sullen teenager, a fretful child.
- Enough to deal with uptightness, irritability, and impatience.
- "Enough to cool the flames of lust, to abate the heights of pride, to appease the itch of covetous desires," as Jeremy Taylor wrote.

"My grace is enough for you," God assures us in 2 Corinthians 12:9.[4] Enough . . . and more than enough.

---

4. The Greek verb usually translated "is sufficient" means "to be enough."

STORMIN' NAAMAN

"Go wash thyself in the Jordan—go, wash thee and be clean!"
Nay, not for any prophet will I plunge a toe therein!

—RUDYARD KIPLING, "NAAMAN'S SONG"

2 Kings 5:1–14

Rabbinic tradition holds that Naaman was the anonymous soldier at the battle of Ramoth Gilead whose "random" shot mortally wounded Ahab, the king of Israel (1 Kings 22:34), and for that reason Syria's victory was attributed to him (2 Kings 5:1). He rose through the ranks to become commander of the army.

Naaman had honor, celebrity, and power, but he was a leper—all lesions and stumps, discolored and deformed, corrupted, shocking in his ugliness, a gross, grisly caricature of what a man was intended to be. Leprosy is one of the most appalling diseases known to humankind. It is treatable today, but in Naaman's day it was terminal. Odd, isn't it, how a little bacillus can bring a big man down?

Of all earth's diseases, leprosy is the only one singled out and linked with sin. It was a "dirty" disease that rendered its victims "unclean," a word that suggests the antithesis of holy.

It's not that leprosy itself was sinful; the disease was rather a metaphor for sin—sin come to the surface. If one could see the fetid, disgusting sight of it, sin would look like an advanced case of leprosy. And, like sin, the end of leprosy is death: Lepers were "cut off from the land of living" and required to wear clothing emblematic of perpetual mourning for the dead (Leviticus 13:45–46). So with sin: We are stone-cold dead in trespasses and sin; "myself, my sepulcher, a moving grave," as John Milton described it.

God had a solution for Naaman's living death. It began with the loving concern of a little girl. We don't know her name. She was just a slave, taken captive from the land of Israel.

The story is necessarily concise; nothing is said about the terror of her abduction, the separation from her family, or the crushing grief of her parents. Nor is there any hint in her of that bitter rage against an adversary that goes by the name of holy zeal. She saw her servitude as an opportunity to serve God in some way. Her occasion came with the serious illness of her master.

Instead of thinking of his disease as justice, she sought help for him, the only help that anyone can give: She wanted to bring him to the living God, where he could find "help . . . in our time of need" (Hebrews 4:16).

She said to her mistress, "If only my master would see the prophet who is in Samaria! He would cure him of his leprosy." The rabbis call attention to the peculiar construction of the sentence and render it, "If only the *supplications* (prayers) of my master could be set before the prophet who is in Samaria." Naaman was a hard man, but underneath there was quiet desperation. He was dying, and there was nothing anyone could do.

Naaman's wife reported the conversation to him, who in turn sought permission from the king to visit Samaria, the capital of Israel. He needed permission and letters of safe conduct, because Israel and Syria were not on friendly terms. The king sent him off with a military escort and a letter to Joram, king of Israel, that said in part, "With this letter I am sending my servant Naaman to you so that you may cure him of his leprosy."

The intent of the letter was to get Naaman in touch with Elisha, as oriental kings were then in close contact with their prophets and priests. The king of Syria assumed that this was the case in Israel and that Joram would simply hand the case over to his prophet.

But Joram had no use for God and His prophet and assumed that everything depended on him. He read the letter, tore his robes, and wailed, "Am I God? Can I kill and bring back to life? Why does this fellow send someone to me to be cured of his leprosy? See how he is trying to pick a quarrel with me!"

Ben-Hadad, the king of Syria, took the girl's words seriously. Joram didn't. The king of Israel, who had the wisdom of the prophets at hand, knew more and believed less than his pagan counterpart.

Somehow Elisha got wind of the matter and sent word to Joram: "Have the man come to me and he will know there is a prophet in Israel." So the great Naaman went with his entourage and summoned the prophet to appear.

Naaman thought the prophet would come out of his house and put on a show—prance and dance, wave his hands over him, shout abracadabra, or make some other hocus-pocus. After all, Naaman was an important man. (The verb translated "surely come" indicates that he thought that Elisha, whom he regarded as his social inferior, had an obligation to come out to meet him. Furthermore, "to me" is in an emphatic position in the sentence suggesting "to someone as important as I!")

But Elisha did not come out to greet Naaman. He simply announced God's word: "Go wash yourself seven times in the Jordan, and your flesh will be restored and you will be cleansed."

Here is double indignity: Elisha not only failed to put in an appearance, but he further humiliated Naaman by insisting that he bathe in Israel's miserable river. Naaman had crossed the Jordan—a gray-green, greasy, sluggish body of water that looked like liquid mud. Indeed, the rivers of Damascus that ran from the snowfields of Lebanon were much more inviting. In outraged pride he stalked away from the Word of God—unchanged.

But Naaman's servants intervened: "My father," they implored, "if the prophet had asked you to do some great thing [literally, if the prophet's word had been a great word], would you not have done it? How much more, then, when he tells you, 'Wash and be cleansed'!"

The text continues: "So he went down and dipped himself in the Jordan seven times, as the man of God had told him, and his flesh was restored and became clean like that of a young boy." The Hebrew text places "and he was clean" last.

A microscopic pathogen, a young girl, certain unknown attendants, and an unassuming prophet were the agents God used to bring about Naaman's humiliation and his cure. His response was worship: "Now I know," he said, "that there is no God in all the world except in Israel."

The reason for the story in its original setting was to establish again the supremacy of Israel's God over all the gods. But I see another meaning: Here in Naaman's leprosy we see a picture of our sin and its cure.

We must "come down" to be healed. As long as we excuse our sin and cling to our rank and nobility, there is nothing God can do. But when we take our place as helpless and undone, when we can say with Edna St. Vincent Millay,

> Mine was the weight
> Of every brooded wrong . . .
> Mine every greed, mine every lust,

then and only then are we are in a place where God by His grace can cleanse us from all our iniquity.

We must fall at His feet. We must confess that we are "dust and ashes and full of sin." Then we are closest to Him, and He is able to set us free from all defilement and make us clean.

Like the flesh "of a young boy." Imagine that! Think of a mighty warrior, with massive muscles rippling beneath the unblemished, unscarred flesh of a little child! This can be ours as well if we allow Jesus to pass His hands over our leprous lives. Though utterly ruined, we can return to the days of our youth—not merely forgiven, but cleansed as if none of our sins had ever occurred; not merely cleansed, but clad in newness of life and in the beauty of our Lord Jesus Christ.

IS THIS
THE TIME?

Is this a time to plant and build,
Add house to house, and field to field?

—JOHN KEBLE, "GEHAZI REPROVED"

aaman, acting on the custom of his country, sought to pay the prophet for his healing. "Please accept now a gift from your servant," he pled. Elisha wanted nothing but God's approval: "As surely as the LORD lives, whom I serve," he replied, "I will not accept a thing." And though Naaman pressed him, he refused.

Israel's prophets frequently accepted offerings (1 Samuel 9:7–8; 1 Kings 14:3), and Elisha had recently received a gift from a countryman (2 Kings 4:42). But it was very important to show this outsider that God's men and women—in contrast to the world's wizards and wise men—give generously without recompense or reward. They expect nothing but God's final, "Well done."

We can scarcely imagine the impression Elisha's refusal had on Naaman and his followers, for their Gentile prophets were driven by greed. But Elisha was motivated by another spirit, that of our Lord who sent His disciples out with this injunction: "Heal the sick, raise the dead, cleanse those who have leprosy, drive out demons. *Freely you have received, freely give*" (Matthew 10:8, italics mine).[1]

Gehazi, however, had another spirit. He said to himself, "My master was too easy on Naaman. . . . As surely as the LORD lives, I will . . . get something for myself." So he hurried after Naaman.

When Naaman saw Gehazi running toward him, he got down from the chariot to meet him. "Is everything all right?" he asked courteously.

---

1. I'm reminded here of Abraham's unwillingness to accept anything from the Hittites and John's remark about the evangelists of his day who "went out for the sake of the Name, accepting nothing from the Gentiles" (3 John 7).

Indeed, Gehazi replied, but "my master Elisha sent me to say, 'Two young men from the company of the prophets have just come to me from the hill country of Ephraim. Please give them a talent of silver and two sets of clothing.' " (Liar, liar, pants on fire!)

"By all means," Naaman replied. *Here, take two talents of silver.* So Gehazi received his silver and sets of clothing, worth several thousand dollars in current exchange, and hid the goods in his house.

When Gehazi entered the prophet's home, Elisha asked: "Where have you been, Gehazi?" he asked.

What? Me? Nowhere.

Ah, but you have been somewhere. Elisha knew what had happened. "Was not my spirit with you when the man got down from his chariot to meet you? Is this the time to take money, or to accept clothes, olive groves, vineyards, flocks, herds, or menservants and maidservants?"

The text says Naaman's disease fell upon Gehazi; he went from Elisha's presence a leper—a ruined man. This is the last we hear of him.

Israel's historian records little that's good about this man, and here you see him at his worst, driven by covetousness, selfishness, and narrow-minded ambition. He was one of Elisha's disciples and lived in close proximity to the prophet, yet he never came into his own, for materialism blinded him to godliness and all that is good.

Greed is a serious affliction, for it draws our hearts away from good. As Jesus put it, "The eye is the lamp of the body. If your eyes are good, your whole body will be full of light. But if your eyes are bad, your whole body will be full of darkness. If then the light within you is darkness, how great is that darkness!" (Matthew 6:22–23).

Put less enigmatically, the ability to discern good and evil is determined by the things on which we focus our gaze. If we set our eyes on money, we may have the good life for a moment, as Gehazi did, but we ourselves will go bad. We'll become confused and uncertain; our judgment will be clouded, and we'll make choices that defy logic and our own long-standing values, choices that may devastate our families and destroy us in the end. As Paul warns us, "People who want to get rich fall into a temptation and a trap and into many foolish and harmful desires that plunge men into ruin and destruction" (1 Timothy 6:9). If we love money we'll go to any lengths to get it, and then . . . "how great is that [moral] darkness."

Jesus does not condemn materialism because it deprives the poor, but because it deprives *us;* we lose our ability to make moral judgments, and like Gehazi we descend into ruin and destruction, a consequence reminiscent of King Midas's golden touch and the misery his greed brought upon himself and his family. "The love of money is a root of all kinds of evil," Paul continues. "Some people, eager for money, have wandered from the faith and pierced themselves with many griefs" (1 Timothy 6:10).

In C. S. Lewis's *Chronicles of Narnia,* Uncle Andrew's greed draws him into the dark arts, and as a result he can no longer see beauty; Edmund's lust for Turkish delight leads him to betray his beloved brothers and sisters to Jadis, the White Witch; Eustace's inordinate desire for dragon gold eventually turns him into a dragon. Greed overcomes Prince Caspian on Deathwater Island as he dreams of the power its magic water will bring him. The other children are drawn to his logic until Aslan erases their memories. They remember only that something terrible has happened in that place and forever after shun it.

As *we* should. Jesus warns us: Beware of greed. "Be on your guard against all kinds of greed; a man's life does not consist in the abundance of his possessions" (Luke 12:15).

> Is this a time to plant and build,
> Add house to house, and field to field?

Tell me, is it?

THE WOULD-BE WOODCUTTER

When I would beget contentment . . . I walk the meadows and there contemplate the little creatures that are cared for by the goodness of God.

—Isaac Walton

2 Kings 6:1–7

God's work, done God's way, is never in vain. If we live and work by faith, and if we endure, there will be those who gather around us and bear fruit for God. "At the proper time we will reap a harvest if we do not give up" (Galatians 6:9).

It may be, in God's providence, that He will enlarge our field of souls and give us greater opportunities. If so, we must receive that gift with thankfulness, humility, meekness, and fear, for it is God who has "done it" (1 Thessalonians 5:24).

So it was with Elisha: God had prospered his work; the number of disciples at Gilgal had swelled to more than a hundred, and their meeting place had become too small. Someone suggested that they go into the woods, cut logs, and enlarge their facilities. Elisha agreed and was invited to accompany the workers.

The party made its way up the Jordan Valley to the spot where they planned to fell trees and float them downriver to the building site. Things were going well until, as Matthew Henry put it, "one of them, accidentally fetching too fierce a stroke (as those who work seldom are apt to be too violent), threw off his axhead into the water."

"Oh, my lord," the man cried, "it was borrowed!"

"Where did it fall?" Elisha asked.

When the man showed Elisha the place, Elisha cut a stick, reached with it into the water, and "made the iron float."

"Lift it out," Elisha said, and "the man reached out his hand and took it."

Some have suggested that nothing miraculous happened, that Elisha simply probed in the water with his stick until he located the axhead and dragged it into sight. That would hardly be worth mentioning, however.

No, it was a miracle: Elisha caused the axhead to "flow," as the text actually says. (The verb occurs in only two other places in the Old Testament: in Lamentations 3:54 (italics added), "waters *flowed* over my head," and in Deuteronomy 11:4, "He made the water of the Red Sea to overflow.") The axhead was set in motion by God's hand and drifted out of deep water into the shallows, where the workman could retrieve it.

The simple miracle enshrines a profound truth: God cares about the small stuff of life—lost axheads, lost coins, lost keys, lost files, lost contact lenses, lost lunker trout, the little things of life that cause us to fret and stew. He does not always restore what was lost (He has good reasons of His own), but He understands our loss and comforts us in our distress.

Next to the assurance of our salvation, the assurance of God's love is essential. Without it we would be alone in the world, exposed to innumerable perils, worries, and fears. It's good to know that He cares; that He is moved by our losses, small as they may be; that our concerns are His concerns as well.

I think of times when my grandchildren have grieved over some small loss, and my heart has been touched by their grief. The broken or mislaid thing had no significance for me—it's usually been some trifling thing—but it wasn't trifling to them. It matters to me, because it matters to them and my grandchildren matter to me.

And so it is with our heavenly Father. Our small worries mean everything to Him, because *we* mean everything to Him. We can cast our care upon Him, *because* He cares about us (1 Peter 5:7).

Annie Johnson Flint has written:

> His grace is great enough to meet the small things,
> The little pin-prick troubles that annoy,
> The insect worries, buzzing and persistent,
> The squeaking wheels that grate upon our joy.

Now I ask you: If God "is great enough to meet the small things," can He not meet the greater things—

> The crashing waves that overwhelm the soul,
> The roaring winds that leave us stunned and breathless,
> The sudden storms beyond life's control.

Can He not give you wisdom in time of confusion? Can He not give comfort in deep sorrow? To quote George MacDonald, if He can "give you all the little things He does not care about . . . will He not help you do the things He wants you to do, but which you do not know how to do?"

Indeed He will—because He cares for you.

MORE OF US

You can observe a lot by seeing.

—YOGI BERRA

2 Kings 6:8–19

D othan was an insignificant settlement about twelve miles north of Israel's capital, Samaria. The city wasn't much to see—about ten acres in size—and there wasn't anything worth defending there; the residents never bothered to build much of a wall. The only defense system in evidence to archaeologists is an unimpressive stone rampart from an earlier period that was pressed into service.

But Dothan was of great interest to Elisha, because Israelites lived there who had not yet bowed the knee to Baal and kissed his feet.

On one occasion Elisha and his servant were ministering at Dothan when Ben-Hadad, the Syrian king, besieged the city in order to kill the prophet. He had good reason to do so, for Elisha had been supplying Israel's King Joram with intelligence about Syrian military movements.

According to Josephus, the Jewish historian, Ben-Hadad had hoped to capture and kill Joram, who frequently hunted along the border between Israel and Syria. (In that era the Jordan valley was heavily wooded and was a prime habitat for lions, bears, and other big game.) Elisha, however, was privy to everything Ben-Hadad planned and kept Joram informed so he was able to avoid being ambushed.

Suspecting skullduggery Ben-Hadad summoned his officers to locate the informant. "Will you not tell me which of us is on the side of the king of Israel?" he shouted.

"None of us, my lord the king," answered an officer, "but Elisha, the prophet who is in Israel, tells the king of Israel the very words you speak in your bedroom."

Ben-Hadad's bedroom was bugged! God overheard the king's pillow-talk each night as he plotted Joram's death. God passed the word on to Elisha who in turn tipped off Joram who thus was able to avoid capture.

"Go, find out where he [Elisha] is," Ben-Hadad thundered in exasperation, "so I can send men and capture him." His officers immediately dispatched a detachment to locate the prophet.

The Syrian scouts quickly discovered that Elisha was residing in Dothan. When they reported the news to Ben-Hadad, he "sent horses and chariots and a strong [LARGE] force." (Big numbers is a typically human notion of power.)

The Syrian army gathered by night, surrounded the city, sized up the situation, decided there was nothing to worry about, and bedded down for the night.

Early the next morning, Elisha's disciple awakened and began making preparations for them to return to their permanent residence in Samaria (see v. 32). He happened to look over the wall and discovered to his dismay that "an army with horses and chariots had surrounded the city." He ran to alert Elisha and cried out in despair, "Oh, my lord, what shall we do?"

"Don't be afraid," Elisha said. "There are more of us than there are of them." Or words to that effect.

Then Elisha prayed, "LORD, open his eyes so he may see." So the Lord opened this young man's eyes: "He looked and saw the hills full of horses and chariots of fire all around Elisha." He saw the legions of heaven at Elisha's disposal, against which Syria's forces were powerless.

Seeing into the unseen world, as I wrote elsewhere, is a mark of maturity. It's an insight that assures us we are never alone. We may feel small and inconsequential in the face of our enemies—they may seem strong and numerous—but there are more on our side than on theirs.

There are those days when, despite Elisha's assurance, we feel vastly outnumbered—in a fraternity where faith seems implausible; in an office where we're badgered and ridiculed; at a fishing lodge where liquor, obscenity, and lies are the norm. Then we recall God's words:

> the chariots of God are tens of thousands
> and thousands upon thousands (Psalm 68:17).

God's enemies (and thus ours) may darken the horizon with innumerable hosts. Like Elisha's servant, we cry out in alarm and complaint to God. But He gives us insight—the vision He showed the prophet of greater armies still, of the armies of the Lord in bright shining armor surrounding the dark and dangerous hosts of evil. We are not alone. God and innumerable angels are encircling us. Though we cannot see them with our natural eyes, they are there! "Surely I am with you always," Jesus assures us, "to the very end of the age" (Matthew 28:20).

Job, surrounded by his troubles and feeling very much alone, mutters to himself,

> If only I knew where to find him;
> if only I could go to his dwelling! (Job 23:3).

He had forgotten that the Lord dwelt in Job's presence; His tent was pitched in the sand by Job's tent.

105

God is with you this moment: in the room in which you read these thoughts, in your car, in your shop, in your office, in deserts, fields, and forests. He could not be nearer if you were now in heaven. You'll see Him there, but He will be no closer in heaven than He is at this moment on earth. As some saint once put it, "His is the Presence in which we have ever been."

Don't fret if you have no sense of His presence. It is no further away than if you felt it. Our Lord pronounced a blessing on those who believe without seeing. He is pleased when you cannot see Him but yet speak to Him as though you were looking into His face. Be still for a moment and say, "He is in *this* place."

This is the truth with which we must meet every circumstance, even those for which we are fully equipped and experienced, and for which we feel wholly adequate. In all situations our sufficiency is not of ourselves, but from God, who alone qualifies and equips us for the work He has called us to do. We must put God between us and all things animate and inanimate that oppose us.

How foolish to arm ourselves with the meager weapons of the flesh—our own limited human resources—when we have the armies of God at our disposal.

> When at length
> the day is through,
> shall I find
> I failed to tap
> the Infinite Resources
> forever open to the weak
> who seek?
>
> —RUTH BELL GRAHAM,
> SITTING BY MY LAUGHING FIRE

We will always seem disadvantaged in this world; our detractors will always appear to outnumber us. Many may rise up against us; many may gather around us in opposition, yet

> the chariots of God are tens of thousands
> and thousands upon thousands.

There are more of us than there are of them![1]

---

1. Permit an afterthought. I am touched by the grace shown to Israel's enemies (2 Kings 6:18–23). When the Syrian army attacked Dothan, God struck every soldier with blindness. Elisha led the blind army to the capital city of Samaria, where Israel's king intended to kill them. The prophet suggested instead that he feed and fete them and send them home—which Joram did. In consequence, Israel's historian reports, Ben-Hadad's efforts to assassinate Joram came to an end. It occurs to me that an awareness of the forces at our disposal may make us gracious to those who oppose us. When God defends us we have no need to defend ourselves. We can turn our energies instead to loving our enemies, as Jesus taught us to do (Matthew 5:43–48).

TRY, TRY, TRY AGAIN

"I am very tired of myself," said the princess. *"But I can't rest until I try again."*

"That is the only way to get rid of your weary, shadowy self, and find your strong, true self. Come, my child; I will help you all I can, for now I can help you."

—George MacDonald, *The Wise Woman*

2 Kings 13:10–19

✦

Jehoash, the king of Israel, came to Elisha to seek his dying counsel. "My father!" he cried, as he bent over the old prophet. "[Where
are] the chariots and horsemen of Israel?"

By this time the army of Israel had been reduced to fifty horsemen, ten chariots, and ten thousand soldiers (2 Kings 13:7). They
were powerless against the Syrian army, which was backed by the
superpower Assyria. With Elisha's death, Jehoash believed that horsemen and chariots of God would depart, and he would be left alone
to face impossible odds.

Elisha responded with a parable, instructing the king to "get a bow
and some arrows." When the king had taken up the weapon, Elisha
"put his hands on the king's hands" and commanded him, "Open the
east window," in the direction of the enemy, and "shoot!"

Shooting an arrow toward an enemy was an ancient way of declar-
ing war. This was also Elisha's way of encouraging Jehoash to take
action, to vigorously prosecute the war against Syria. And by placing his hands on the young king's hands, the prophet assured Jehoash
that the strength of the shot came from the Lord, just as a man might
put his hands on a child's hands and pull a bow too powerful for him
to draw.

Then Elisha sealed the symbol with the prediction that the king
and his army would defeat Syria in battle. "The Lord's arrow of vic-

tory, the arrow of victory over Aram!" Elisha declared. "You will completely destroy the Arameans [Syrians] at Aphek."

But there was more. Elisha told the king to take arrows from his quiver and shoot into the ground. Jehoash did so three times and then stopped.

Elisha was indignant. "You should have struck the ground five or six times," meaning, you should have shot all the arrows in your quiver, "then you would have defeated Aram and completely destroyed it. But now you will defeat it only three times."

And so it was: "Jehoash son of Jehoahaz recaptured from Ben-Hadad son of Hazael the towns he had taken in battle from his father Jehoahaz. *Three times* Jehoash defeated him" (2 Kings 13:25, italics mine).

Most of us will never do battle with Syrians, but we're all engaged in unending struggle with "sinful desires, which war against [the] soul" (1 Peter 2:11)—an uncontrolled temper, an alcohol or drug addiction, a sexual perversion, a tendency toward sloth, greed, malice, bitterness, or sullen pride.

The first step is to declare war against the enemy. We must never give in to a sinful habit that has taken up residence in us. We must declare war! There can be no neutrality and no surrender. We must *never* make peace with the flesh. To do so is to invite disaster. We will master sin or be mastered by it. There is no middle ground.

The second step is to remind ourselves that God is a hands-on God. It is by His power and might that we are set free. Without *Him* we do *nothing*.

And finally, we must never give up. We must keep drawing the bow; keep striking a blow! It is through faith and patience that we receive the promise. If nothing else, our struggle against sin will cause us to turn to God again and again and cling to Him in desperation, which may, in the end, be worth more to God than present deliverance, for what He wants most of all is our dependence and love.

It may be that our struggle will continue until death, or until the Lord comes—certainly there will be times when we will get discouraged—but we must never give up.

As John White writes in his book *The Fight:*

> There is no place for giving up. The warfare is so much bigger than our personal humiliations. To feel sorry for oneself is totally inappropriate. Over such a soldier I would pour a bucket of icy water. I would drag him to his feet, kick him in the rear end, put a sword in his hand, and shout, "Now fight!" In some circumstances one must be cruel to be kind. What if you have fallen for a tempting ruse of the Enemy? What if you're not the most brilliant swordsman in the army? You hold Excalibur in your hand! Get behind the lines for a break if you're too weak to go on, strengthen yourself with a powerful draught of the wine of Romans 8:1–4. Then get back into the fight before your muscles get stiff!

What's required is dogged endurance through the ebbs and flows, ups and downs, victories and losses of life, knowing that God is working in us to accomplish His purpose. We must staunchly, steadfastly, persistently pursue God's will until we stand before Him and His work is done.

God is dogged in His endurance as well, and He is wonderfully persistent: He will *never* give up on us!

"No amount of falls can really undo us," C. S. Lewis wrote, "if we keep picking ourselves up each time. We shall, of course, be very muddy and tattered children by the time we reach home. . . . The only fatal thing is to lose one's temper and give up."

> When things go wrong, as they sometimes will,
>   When the road you are trudging seems all uphill . . .

When care is pressing you down a bit,
 Rest if you must, but don't you quit. . . .

You never can tell how close you are,
 It may be near when it seems afar.
So stick to the fight when you are hardest hit,
 It is when things seem worst that you must not quit.

—AUTHOR UNKNOWN

THE DEAD PROPHET'S
SOCIETY

Throughout [Elisha's] life no ruler could shake him,
  and no one could subdue him.
No task was too hard for him,
  and even in death his body prophesied.
In his lifetime he performed wonders,
  and in his death his works were marvellous.

— ECCLESIASTICUS 48:12–14, *JERUSALEM BIBLE*

2 Kings 13:20–21

Elisha died, but that's not the end of his story.

Sometime later, when certain Israelites were burying the body of a dead friend, a band of Moabite raiders appeared on the horizon. The Israelites spied a nearby tomb—Elisha's tomb it turned out—rolled the stone from the entrance, cast the corpse into the grave, and fled.

The moment the dead body touched Elisha's bones, the dead Israelite "came to life and stood up on his feet," and, I suppose, fled alongside his friends. (Imagine their surprise!) Perhaps he escaped the raid, for, according to an old legend, he lived many years and fathered a large number of sons and daughters.

What can we make of this odd miracle at the end of the account of Elisha's story? What message lies buried with the prophet? How does his body yet prophesy?

In its original setting, the story rounds off the author's Baal polemic and makes the argument that a dead prophet of Yahweh has more power than a living prophet of Baal. But then that's true of all of God's workers. Our best work is done postmortem.

Paul put it this way: "We always carry around in our body the death of Jesus, so that the life of Jesus may also be revealed in our body. For we who are alive are always being given over to death for Jesus' sake, so that his life may be revealed in our mortal body. So then, death is at work in us, but life is at work in you" (2 Corinthians 4:10–12).

We must ponder the apostle's words. "We who are alive are *always* being given over to death." We are in deaths *often* (2 Corinthians 11:23); we die many deaths every day.

We pray to be relevant in our proclamation of the truth, and our words fall unheeded to the ground. We ask to be useful and helpful, and we're unnoticed and deemed unnecessary. We long to do a great work, and we find ourselves in a low and narrow place. We labor with integrity and skillful hands, and ungodly men and women obstruct and frustrate us and eventually take our work away. Our reputations suffer; we long for justice, and vindication is delayed. We're disquieted by our difficulties and dilemmas, and there seems no way to resolve them. We're hurt by the insensitivity or indifference of our friends. We get old and obsolete, and folks think we're of no use any longer.

This is "death at work in us," grinding us down, diminishing us, until we have no confidence in the flesh, until we learn that our background, education, experience, intelligence, personality, age, and appearance have no power in themselves. Nothing in us is a source of hope, nothing is worth defending, nothing is special or admirable. There is nothing left but to fall into the ground and die.

This is what Paul means when he says, "We always carry around in our bodies the death [literally, 'the dying'] of Jesus." It's not easy to do, but we endeavor to adopt *Jesus'* attitude toward dying.

Our Lord died every day of His life and many times every day. The cross was but the culmination of an entire lifetime of dying. When insulted, misrepresented, rejected, misunderstood, He quietly submitted to His Father's will: "Not my will, but yours be done" (Luke 22:42). This must be our response as well.

Death brings us to the end of ourselves. It strips us of our self-assurance, and the assets on which we normally rely, so we will rely solely upon God. Paul writes of his sufferings in Asia and explains the process this way: "In our hearts we felt the sentence of death. But this happened that we might not rely on ourselves but on God, who raises the dead" (2 Corinthians 1:9).

Death is the path of human existence, but death is not meaningless. Simultaneously with death a richer life begins to emerge, a life that can be described only as the "life of Christ," a quality of life that manifests itself in the meekness with which we accept criticism, the uncomplaining spirit with which we endure long-term illness, the love we give to cold indifference, the patience with which we respond to repeated provocation, the endurance we display in the presence of intense and mean-spirited opposition, the kindness we show to those who have wronged us.

This is the mysterious, invisible life of Jesus made visible in our mortal flesh, communicating reality and vitality to others. Our friends see His life manifest in us and long to be made alive, to experience the life that God has worked in us.

This is a mystery, impossible to produce by self-effort and difficult to explain. I can describe it only as Paul does: "So then, death is at work in us, but life is at work in you." Dying brings a richer life. Those who have died and come to life leave behind a harvest of righteousness wherever we go.

And, I hasten to add, the results of our lives need not end with our earthly existence. Our influence may outlive us, lingering on through the things we have spoken or written and through the fragrance of our lives. God may use all that He has worked in us for the enrichment of souls for years to come, perhaps until He comes again. As old growth falls to the ground, its individuality lost and forgotten, new growth may spring out of the old, born out of its life and nourished by it. God only knows the possibilities that lie within us when we are willing to die.

In her nature-based *Parables of the Cross,* Lilias Trotter wrote,

> God may use . . . the things that He has wrought in us for the blessing of souls unknown to us: as these twigs and leaves of bygone years,

whose originality is forgotten, pass on vitality still to the newborn wood sorrel. God only knows the endless possibilities that lie folded in each one of us. Shall we not go to all lengths with Him in His plans for us—not, as these "green things upon the earth" in their unconsciousness, but with the glory of free choice? Shall we not translate the story of their little lives into our own?

"Will it work for me?" you ask. It has worked for centuries for all who are willing to abandon themselves to God's will. Not in the same way with everyone, of course, for our Father deals with us according to His infinite and intimate understanding of our souls, souls He created and thus knows better than we do. He knows the path we must take to be conformed to the image of His Son. He is at work both to will and to do of His good pleasure. "My Father is always at his work to this very day," Jesus said (John 5:17), working every day and in every circumstance to bring us to the fullness of Christ.

What an incentive to holiness! To know that He will not give up on us until we are perfect—like Him! He is faithful, and He will do it.

A seed is no good when it lies on the ground. As Jesus put it, it must "fall *into* the ground and die. But if it dies, it produces many seeds" (John 12:24 KJV, NIV, italics mine). This is His guarantee.

As with Elisha, our death is not the end of the story.

Note to the Reader

The publisher invites you to share your response to the message of this book by writing Discovery House Publishers, Box 3566, Grand Rapids, MI 49501, USA. For information about other Discovery House books, music, or videos, contact us at the same address or call 1-800-653-8333. Find us on the Internet at http://www.dhp.org; or send e-mail to books@dhp.org.